SENECA RAY STODDARD

Adirondack Illustrator

SENECA RAY STODDARD:
Adirondack Illustrator

by
William Crowley

An Exhibition at the Adirondack Museum
Blue Mountain Lake, New York
June 15 to October 15, 1981 & 1982

Front Cover: *Avalanche Lake, Adirondacks,* © 1888.
Back Cover: *High Art, Blue Mountain, Sept. 15, 1879,* Stoddard with portable darkroom.

ISBN: 0-910020-35-3
Library of Congress catalog card number: 82-071968
Published by the Adirondack Museum of the Adirondack Historical Association.
2,000 copies of this catalog were printed by Canterbury Press, Rome, New York.
Typeset in 11/13 Optima Roman.
Design by G. Robert Reynolds.

Table of Contents

Acknowledgments vii

An Adirondack Career 1

Landscape Photography 13

References 22

Figures 16–20 24–27

Plates 1–30 28–57

Checklist of the Exhibition 58–62

Chronology 63–64

Acknowledgments

THIS EXHIBIT AND CATALOG would not have been possible without the assistance and research of many people. Almost all the images and artifacts are from the Adirondack Museum's library and curatorial collections. In twenty-five years the museum has assembled the largest single collection of Stoddard material anywhere, centering on 5,000 to 6,000 photographs but including several hundred books, manuscripts, maps, drawings and paintings as well. Several staff members helped to build the Stoddard Collection, but William K, Vener and Edward Comstock deserve special credit for selecting approximately 3,600 Stoddard items acquired by the museum, with funds from the Adirondack Historical Association, between 1974 and 1977. Most of these items came from Maitland DeSormo who purchased the major body of Stoddard's work from the photographer's family in 1962.

Lenders to the exhibition include the Chapman Historical Museum of Glens Falls, Wildwood Enterprises, Mr. and Mrs. William K. Verner and Mr. and Mrs. Robert Worth. Joan Youngken, of the Chapman Historical Museum, which also has a large Stoddard collection, was particularly helpful in sharing her research on the photographer. The museum is indebted to the Carl E. Plumley family for the purchase of the Stoddard painting "The Narrows, Lake George." Special thanks are due to Mr. and Mrs. Adam Hochschild who donated a unique elephant folio album of photographs that Stoddard had presented to William West Durant about 1889 and which Durant, years later, gave to Harold K. Hochschild, the founder of the Adirondack Museum.

This catalog could not have been published without the support and assistance of many current staff members. Craig and Alice Gilborn read several drafts of the manuscript and contributed editorial advice. The ideas and expressions are the author's, who assumes responsibility for errors or omissions. Judy Valentine spent many hours at the microfilm reader looking for newspaper references on Stoddard. Dorothy Swanson patiently typed numerous versions of the catalog. Tracy Meehan deserves special thanks for long hours of searching the collections, helping to organize and mount the exhibition and contributing thoughtful advice throughout the project.

William Crowley, *Curator*
Adirondack Museum
Blue Mountain Lake, N.Y.

An Adirondack Career

SENECA RAY STODDARD spent most of his adult life writing about and illustrating the Adirondacks. From his studio and home in Glens Falls, a principal gateway to the region from the south, he both encouraged and cashed in on the burgeoning tourist trade which flourished in the years following the Civil War. Through guidebooks and paintings and, later, through maps, souvenir booklets, lectures, magazines and especially photographs, Stoddard built his career on the emerging recreational industry. He was also an early and vocal supporter of the movement to protect the Adirondack wilderness from the lumberman and preserve its natural character for future generations. In the process, he left a strong visual document of the Adirondacks from 1870 to 1910 — a crucial time in the history of the area.

Prior to the Civil War, the Adirondack mountains were the preserve of a few fur trappers, hunters, lumbermen and occasional sportsmen. Towns and villages had grown up on the perimeter of the region, but settlements in the interior were few and widely scattered. Most of the area was still wilderness.

The situation changed dramatically after the war. The frontier was rapidly disappearing while industrial and commercial growth was leading to increasing urbanization. Americans were becoming aware of the shrinking wilderness and the recreational potential of the natural environment.

The Rev. William H. H. Murray was among the first to write about the Adirondacks from the viewpoint of the sportsman and tourist. The publication of his *Adventures in the Wilderness,* in the spring of 1869, had an immediate impact upon the region. Hundreds and then thousands of vacationers soon were visiting the Adirondacks each summer. Railroads, stage and steamboat lines, and hotels sprung up to accommodate the throngs of visitors.[1] We know that Stoddard had read Murray's book by 1874 and that he also recognized the area's recreational potential.[2] Even more than Murray, Stoddard was a major influence upon the development of the Adirondack tourist economy which characterizes the region to this day.

Born on May 13, 1843 in the Town of Wilton, Saratoga County, New York, Seneca Ray Stoddard (figure 1) was a member of the farm family of Charles and Julia Stoddard. We know little about his early life or whether he received any formal training in the arts. About 1862, at the age of 19 he took a job as an ornamental painter of railroad cars with the firm of Eaton and Gilbert in Troy, N.Y.[3] In 1864 he moved to Glens Falls and opened a shop for "House, Sign, and Ornamental Paint-

Figure 1. Seneca Ray Stoddard, n.d.

ing."[4] Thus began a career in the visual arts which would stretch over the next 50 years.

Stoddard gradually moved into the fields of portrait and landscape work (figures 2 & 16). He was listed as a "landscape painter" in the 1870 census, and several notices regarding his paintings appeared in the local papers at that time.[5,6] He also offered art lessons in his studio on Elm Street.[7] However, as he moved into publishing and photography, he seems to have stopped painting entirely.

His landscape paintings, while charming, show a lack of technical skill. He was more successful with his sketches and drawings which have a refreshing spontaneity that he was unable to convey in oils on canvas

Figure 2. *View at Dresden,* n.d., probably Stoddard's easel.

(figure 17). Stoddard continued to use his sketches and drawings to illustrate his guidebooks well into the 1890s (figure 19).

This early experience in the graphic arts had an important effect upon his later career, if only to sharpen his interest in the natural beauties of the Adirondacks. Furthermore, he undoubtedly learned some of the basic principles of composition which served him so well when he began to use the camera to depict nature.

Exactly when Stoddard began using a camera or how he learned the relatively new technique is unknown. He must have mastered the basic processes by 1867, for the following notice appeared in the *Glens Falls Republican* in that year:

> Mr. S. R. Stoddard, Photographer, has taken a number of instantaneous sterreoscopic [sic] views of natural objects in this vicinity, and especially about our beautiful falls, which are not only interesting and valuable to residents here, but possess real merit as a collection of scenery hardly excelled by those produced from any locality in the United States. He has also photographed our banks and churches and several private dwellings . . . Mr. S. has chosen his objects with the eye of an artist, and his work is well and faithfully done.[8]

It is interesting to note that these early images were outdoor views. Most professional photographers at this time limited their work to portraits done within the confines of the studio. Outdoor photography entailed considerable difficulty due to the bulky equipment and the heavy glass plate negatives which had to be developed in the field. Nonetheless, Stoddard's earlier interest in landscape art drew him in the direction of outdoor photography — a field he would specialize in for the rest of his career.

Figure 3. Stoddard's Logo, n.d., Courtesy of the Chapman Historical Museum.

Still listed as an artist in the 1870 census, Stoddard seems to have adopted photography as his primary profession shortly thereafter. By 1874 he was able to offer over 600 stereo views and 200 larger prints for sale.[9] As early as 1871 the nation's largest photographic sales firm, E. & H. T. Anthony & Company of New York City, was offering Stoddard views of Lake George as part of their Christmas selection.[10] In 1873 he portrayed himself in a satirical logo (figure 3), with the following explanation;

> Well, that's Stoddard, the photographer, and that's his boat, the WANDERER. He wanders around all over the lake, taking views and money. Notice that picture on his sail, looking more like cancer in the old-fashioned almanacs than anything else that I can think of? Well, he calls that his "coat of arms" — *Legs* would be more appropriate — and it is supposed to be himself astride a camera (his hobby) in pursuit of wealth, there represented by a fat-looking money bag with wings, to show the nature of the game he hopes to bring down by aid of his lance, that being, as he also claims to be an artist, a mahl stick.[11]

Stoddard's early photographs were mostly taken in the villages of Glens Falls and Saratoga Springs or along the fringes of the Adirondacks at such places as Lake George, Fort Ticonderoga, and Lake Champlain. His first trip into the interior of the Adirondacks was in the fall of 1870.[12] According to a newspaper account of that year, Stoddard took a camera as well as his sketchbook along on the trip.[13] While no prints from this journey have been identified, it is clear from surviving photographs that he was using a camera on his second visit to the interior of the region in 1873 (figure 4).

From that point on, Stoddard increasingly concentrated his efforts upon the Adirondacks. Over the next forty years he produced thousands of images of the region, estimated by one collector to number more than 10,000 photographs.[14] As early as 1876 he was offering "2,000 different views" of the area.[15] The Adirondack Museum's collection contains approximately 5,000–6,000 distinct images.

Whatever the exact number, it is obvious that he spent the major portion of his career as a pictorial chronicler of the Adirondacks. Most of his photographs were frankly aimed at the tourist trade. Several generations of vacationers are shown hunting, camping, fishing, boating and hiking in the Adirondacks. A perusal of his images allows us to follow these people throughout their trips to the area: we travel with them on the steamboats, railroads and stagecoaches that brought them to the mountains, and we see the elegant hotels and humble boarding houses in which they stayed. The observer joins them around the campfire and sees the same magnificent vistas of mountains and lakes that drew them to the area.

Figure 4. *Whiteface Mountain — "Three Braves," Oct. 3, 1873.* S. R. Stoddard on right.

Nor did Stoddard forget local residents. Crusty guides, tough lumbermen, wealthy entrepreneurs and genial hotel keepers were all depicted by his camera. In sum, Stoddard provided the tourists with souvenirs of their trip and the arm chair traveler with a vicarious visit to the Adirondacks.

Stoddard used a variety of means to sell his photographs both locally and nationally. The first mention of his photos, in an 1867 issue of a Glens Falls newspaper, stated that his views were on sale at the local bookstores.[16] In 1874 he began advertising his images in his guidebooks, and a year later he published his first photographic catalog.[17] The same 1874 advertisement states that his views were also available on board several Adirondack steamboats and in many hotels.[18] In 1884 Stoddard actually leased the newsstands on two steamboats and at several hotels.[19] A perusal of his account books indicates that he received orders from all over the country.[20]

In addition to his work for the general tourist trade, Stoddard also accepted several special photographic assignments. In 1878 he was hired by Verplank Colvin to take charge of the photographic division of the New York State Topographical Survey of the Adirondacks (figure 5). It is interesting to note that Colvin began mapping the region at about the same time as the major scientific expeditions to the American West. Stoddard made approximately 200 views for the survey, primarily 360 °panoramas taken from Adirondack mountain tops.[21]

Like many other landscape photographers of his day, Stoddard was employed by railroad companies to depict their lines and advertise the attractions of the territory through which the traveler would pass. As early as 1881 he photographed the route of the New York and Canadian Railroad along Lake Champlain (figure 6).[22] He also worked for the Adirondack Railroad Company and the Central Vermont Railway.

An ardent canoeist, Stoddard combined business with pleasure. In the early 1880s he joined the newly formed American Canoe Association and attended many of their annual meetings held at Lake George, Lake Champlain and in the Thousand Islands of the St. Lawrence River.

Figure 5. *Adirondack Survey Signal on Noon Mark, Oct. 1, 1878.*

His photographs of the organization's activities appeared in A.C.A. yearbooks and were sold separately (figure 7). Stoddard also published several souvenir booklets entitled, *Glimpses of the A.C.A.*[23]

Commissions from private individuals provided another source of income. Perhaps his best customers were Dr. Thomas Clark Durant and his son William West Durant, wealthy Adirondack land developers. In addition to his work for the Durants' Adirondack Railroad, Stoddard produced photographic albums of camps Pine Knot and Sagamore for them (plate 25).[24] The Adirondack Museum owns an elephant folio album of Adirondack photographs, each measuring 14½" by 18½", which Stoddard made especially for W. W. Durant. Other wealthy Adirondack patrons included Robert C. Pruyn and Collis P. Huntington.[25]

One project particularly close to Stoddard's heart was his work for the New York State Forest Commission. On

Figure 6. *Photographic Special 1881, N.Y. & C.R.R.*

February 25, 1892, at the invitation of the Commission, Stoddard presented an illustrated lecture to the New York State Assembly in Albany urging passage of a bill to create an "Adirondack Park." His hand-tinted lantern slides eloquently illustrated the region he wished to see preserved for further generations.[26] On several other occasions the Forest Commission used his images in its annual reports.[27] In 1892, for example, this state agency ordered 42,000 prints from Stoddard.[28] His work also appeared in a number of books and such magazines as *Harper's Weekly* and *Frank Leslie's Illustrated Newspaper.*[29]

At first, most of Stoddard's photographs were sold individually or in sets of stereographs. Beginning in 1878, however, he adopted a variety of lithographic and photomechanical means to reproduce his images in bound sets of views. These "art books," as Stoddard called them, contained a selection of his most popular

Figure 7. *A.C.A. Camp, 1887, Springfield.*

views and were usually accompanied by descriptive or historical text.[30]

The Chapman Historical Society, of Glens Falls, has in its collections a bound volume, entitled *Ausable Chasm,* which contains original Stoddard albumen prints. Although he used original prints to illustrate a view book on at least one other occasion, Stoddard found this type of photographic reproduction time consuming and expensive.[31] In 1878 he published a small "souvenir album of the Adirondacks" containing 32 lithographic reproductions of his photographs.[32] Eventually he published over forty of these souvenir albums, most of which illustrate and describe Adirondack subjects.

Perhaps the most intriguing of the view books is *Lake George,* published in 1883 and containing "artotype illustrations" by Edward Bierstadt.[33] It is unclear whether some of the photographs are by Bierstadt, or whether Stoddard was giving a fellow photographer credit for the use of Bierstadt's patented collotype printing process. In any case, it is interesting to note that Stoddard was in contact with another of the noted landscape photographers of his day.[34]

Not all of Stoddard's work was confined to the Adirondacks. From the beginning, he had recorded town scenes and landscapes along the Hudson River and in other parts of New York State. During the summers of 1883 to 1886 he covered, in stages, the distance from Glens Falls to St. Johns, New Brunswick, in a sailing canoe.[35] His first illustrated lecture was based on photographs taken during these trips.[36] In later years he traveled to Florida, Alaska, the American West and Europe to gather material for other lectures. The lengths he would go to obtain his photographs is exemplified by his trip to the Mediterranean in 1895, when he concealed a camera in his bedroll in order to capture unwilling subjects on film (figure 8).

True to the entrepreneurial spirit of the times, Stoddard was continually looking for new sources of income

Figure 8. *The Man with the Kovered Kodak,* 1895. Stoddard with hidden camera.

based upon his photographic skills. In 1882 he was granted a patent for a photographic plate holder, which was manufactured and distributed by E. L. Elliot and Co., of Auburn, N.Y.[37] In the 1890s he became a distributor for Kodak film and cameras.[38] In later years, he offered developing and printing services as well as instructions for amateurs.[39] Despite these forays into other fields and to distant lands, the majority of his photographs depict the Adirondacks and the illustration of this region constituted his life's work.

However, it was not only through his photographs that Stoddard portrayed and publicized the Adirondacks. As tourists began coming in numbers to the region, Stoddard recognized a need and market for a publication which would help the rising tide of vacationers plan their trip to the Adirondacks. Beginning in 1873, he brought out a series of guidebooks which he revised annually until 1914 or 1915.

The first of these guidebooks was entitled *Lake George; (Illustrated.) A Book of To-Day.* It contained practical information about hotel accommodations and transportation routes plus historical material on the area. Its success is indicated by the fact that the first printing of 1,000 copies was quickly followed by a second edition of 3,000 in August, 1873.[40] At the same time, Stoddard published a second guidebook, *Ticonderoga: Past and Present.* In 1874 he combined the two into one volume which covered Lake George, Saratoga, Luzerne and Schroon Lake. In 1887 he added material on Lake Champlain. From that time on this book provided the basic core of information for subsequent, revised guides to the eastern Adirondacks. During the 1880s and 1890s he included a large fold out map of Lake George with the guidebook.

Stoddard made his second trip into the interior of the Adirondacks in the fall of 1873. Accompanied by his brother-in-law, Charles Oblenis, he traveled throughout the Adirondacks sketching and photographing the area and taking descriptive notes.[41] These notes, written in narrative form, served as the basis of his most popular guidebook, *The Adirondacks: Illustrated,* published in 1874 (figure 19). The back of the book contained lists of guides, the distances involved in a variety of trips, modes of transportation and fares, and information on hotel and boarding house accommodations. As was the case with his other guidebooks, this information was revised annually but the basic narrative remained the same until 1893. In that year, Stoddard dropped the narrative in favor of a more factual description of routes, transportation facilities and accommodations. In 1895 both the guidebooks were published in a more convenient "pocket sized" edition. Although he produced a series of maps to accompany this guide, they were not included in the price of the publication.

Stoddard seems to have been influenced by the humorous writing of Mark Twain, particularly Twain's *Innocents Abroad* in which the author himself, and the American tourist in general, is the object of numerous jokes. Take, for example, Stoddard's description of his lanky appearance and less than energetic work habits;

> . . . nature was very lavish in the bestowal of longitude, although not noticeably so in regard to latitude, giving also a disposition to dare, and a physical development capable of enduring a vast amount of arduous rest.[42]

Unlike Murray, Stoddard did not seem to have been very interested in either hunting or fishing. The following description of eating fish-balls at Paul Smith's Hotel is a marvelous satire of Murray's book and typical of Stoddard's antic style;

> Ah! Can it be possible? Yes, *yes,* it is! It is!! A school of fish-balls within easy reach! I will catch one; but what true fisherman can act the part of the butcher? True greatness in that line consists not in the amount bagged, but the manner of doing it. . . . I prepared for a cast. A moment's hesitation, in which the momentous question presented itself whether I had better take my "scarlet dragon" or "blue-tailed ibes." I tried both, but not a ripple stirred the quiet depths; then I tried a spoon. . . . Carefully I played it around over the bread; dragged it slowly across the potatoes, skittered it lightly over the butter and let it drop where I knew the wary creatures were lying in wait. Slowly it settled down, lightly as the dew into the the heart of a blushing rose. A gentle ripple stirred the surface; I felt intuitively that the trying moment had come. A thrill shot up my arm and throughout my body to the very pit of my stomach as the beautiful creature curled upward and struck — struck hard. Then began the struggle for life . . .[43]

We do not know how many copies of the guidebooks Stoddard sold in his lifetime. The two major guides were undoubtedly popular, for each was revised annually and went through over forty editions. Alfred L. Donaldson, an early historian of the Adirondacks, claimed that *The Adirondacks: Illustrated* was by far the most widely consulted guidebook of the region.[44] They were sold through the mails, in hotels and resorts and in many bookstores throughout the eastern United States. Judging from the comments of bookstore owners and newspaper reviews, the books seem to have been widely known and well received.[45]

No travelers guide would be complete without a map, and Stoddard was not remiss in recognizing and fulfilling this need. In 1874 he published a *Map of the New York Wilderness* to accompany the *Adirondacks Illustrated.* It is unclear whether or not this map was included in the price of the guidebook or was sold separately. Although Stoddard's name appeared on the map it was actually a copy of William W. Ely's map first published in 1867.[46]

In 1880 Stoddard compiled and published a completely new map entitled, *Map of the Adirondack Wilderness* (figure 18). Although much of the information was based upon previous maps and the reports of surveyors, land developers, guides, and hotel keepers, this map was an original production, not a copy of previous work.[47] The distinguishing characteristic of the map was its circular format which allowed Stoddard to show "air-line" distances from Mt. Marcy. Providing information on railroads, roads, trails and carries, its usefulness for the potential tourist is apparent. Donaldson called it the most popular tourist map of the Adirondacks.[48]

Stoddard published this map of the Adirondacks, with minor revisions, from 1880 to at least 1908. Although intended for use with his guidebook, the maps were sold separately. In 1888 Stoddard printed a special edition of the map for the New York State Forest Commission. Sometime between 1908 and 1912 he issued an entirely new version of the map which abandoned the circular format and added information on ". . . distances in miles and tenths of miles by approved auto routes from New York City."[49] In 1909 or 1910 he published an *Auto-Road Map of the Adirondacks, the Champlain Valley and the Hudson River* which covered the eastern part of the region.[50] Obviously, Stoddard was capable of changing with the times and catering to the emerging boom in automobile travel.

In 1880, while his new map of the Adirondacks was being published, Stoddard was also conducting a survey of Lake George and the surrounding territory. The result was a separate *Map of Lake George* based on "surveys of 1880 by S. R. Stoddard."[51] Apparently this map was first issued in 1881 and was approved and adopted by the New York State Engineer and Surveyor for a report on public lands issued in 1883.[52] This large color map, 38" by 10¾", was available from 1881 to at least 1913. It was sold separately at first, but was included in the price of the Lake George guidebook, from 1888 to 1901.

In 1890 Stoddard published a *Map of Lake Champlain* which also included inset maps of Lake George, the Richelieu River in Canada and transportation routes to several interior resorts.[53] Approximately the same size and format as the Lake George map, it was sold separately and was available until at least 1914.

Perhaps Stoddard's most ambitious cartographic effort was his hydrographic *Chart of Lake George.* This map was based on topographic surveys and depth soundings of the lake conducted between 1906 and 1908. Showing the depths of Lake George, locating "rocks and dangerous reefs," and indicating all points with less than six feet of water, the chart was invaluable to sportsmen and steamboat operators.[54] Portions of the map were issued in 1907 and the entire chart, measuring 8 feet by 15 inches, was first published in 1909.[55]

Thus, Stoddard added surveying and cartographic skills to his abilities as a writer and photographer. These talents were primarily turned to the task of publicizing and describing the Adirondacks to the potential tourist.

There remained yet one more skill which Stoddard added to his repertoire for promoting the region and enhancing his income. On February 12, 1891 he presented an illustrated lecture in Glens Falls with the title "A Canoe Trip to the Bay of Fundy."[56] In following years he developed lectures on the Adirondacks, the Hudson River, and such distant lands as the American West, Alaska, the Mediterranean and Scandinavia.[57] As early as 1893 he seems to have acquired an agent, Major J. B. Pond, of the Star Lyceum Bureau in New York City, who arranged for speaking engagements throughout the country.[58] In the years 1900 to 1902 he was a regular speaker at the Florida Chautauqua in DeFuniak Springs.[59] These lectures were illustrated by hand-tinted glass lantern slides projected upon a large screen.

The lecture closest to Stoddard's heart and the one that probably launched his career as a public speaker, was his presentation to the New York State Assembly in February, 1892. There he spoke out against and graphically illustrated the damage lumbermen were doing in the Adirondacks, particularly the damming of rivers and the creation of drowned lands (plate 30). He advocated a ban on cutting evergreens above 1,500 feet in elevation and argued passionately for the passage of a bill creating the Adirondack Park.[60] Following his presentation to the Assembly, Stoddard toured the state speaking in favor of the legislation. We will never be able to assess the importance of his individual efforts, but the bill did pass the legislature and became law on May 20th of that year.

Stoddard had first written about his concern for protecting the Adirondack environment in an article published in *Outing* magazine in 1885.[61] Even after the creation of the Park he continued to speak out against the lumber companies and in favor of a variety of laws banning their more destructive practices.[62]

His continuing concern for the environment led to his one unsuccessful venture. In May, 1906, he began publication of a magazine titled *Stoddard's Northern Monthly* (figure 20). The purposes of the periodical were clearly stated in the October issue:

> Pictures talk. Stoddard's Northern Monthly. For picturing with pen and camera the glories of the Adirondack mountains. For the gathering and preservation of its unrecorded stories and traditions. For the saving of "The Great North Woods" and the advancement of its broader human interests, is the mission of Stoddard's Northern Monthly.[63]

Despite the high purposes and lavish illustrations of the early issues, the magazine was never a financial success. In the August, 1908 issue he wrote that the *Monthly* would cease publication due to the lack of subscribers.[64]

In any case, Stoddard had just passed his sixty-eighth birthday and was beginning to curtail what had been a busy and productive life. Although he lived for another nine years and continued to publish and revise his guidebooks and maps, he seems to have cut back on his photography and travel.

Stoddard's career had been intimately identified with the Adirondacks. He had illustrated them through maps, guidebooks, paintings, photographs and lectures. Although there is no denying that his foremost consideration was to earn a livelihood from the tourist trade, he also had a deep respect for the Adirondacks and did much to preserve them for future generations.

His photographs have stood the test of time better than any of his other illustrative efforts. His images provide a prolific visual record of the region during a formative period in its history, 1870–1910, when the area was in transition from a subsistence and extractive economy to a society increasingly dependent on the tourist trade — an economy which still characterizes the Adirondacks. Stoddard encouraged and documented this critical change. Perhaps his career was best summed up in 1894 by the New York *Mail and Express:*

> Close upon the heels of Murray came S. R. Stoddard with his camera, his notebook and his brush, all of which he used to make the fame of the Adirondack wilderness known to the outside world. Stoddard has done even more than Murray to publish the results of his discoveries for in his guidebooks, on his maps, on the lecture platform, on the screen, in poetry and in song, he has for more than a quarter of a century preached the Adirondacks and them glorified.[65]

Landscape Photography

STODDARD'S GREATEST ACHIEVEMENT was as a photographer of outdoor and landscape subjects. He seems to have been interested in recording the natural environment from the time he began using a camera. The earliest notice of his photographic work, quoted previously, praised his "collection of scenery" taken in 1867. In 1874 he was listed as a "landscape photographer" in the Glens Falls directory.[66] His study of a marsh on Lake Champlain dates from that year (figure 9). Throughout his career the vast majority of his images portrayed outdoor subjects. This was not typical of photographers in his day, most of whom did portrait work and rarely took their equipment out of the studio.

During much of the nineteenth century, any photographer who took a camera into the field faced considerable technical problems. This was especially true in the era of the first photographic process, the daguerreotype. Introduced in 1839, the technique depended on the use of a silver coated copper plate and required exposures of up to thirty minutes, which meant that movement by the subject would ruin the image. More importantly, it was a direct positive process from which no duplicates could be made; even if one were to overcome the technical problems of using a daguerrian camera in the field, it

Figure 9. *Marsh, Lake George,* © 1874.

was impossible to produce and sell multiple copies and recoup expenses.[67]

The first practical solution to the problem, the wet plate negative, was introduced into this country about 1855. This process used a collodion solution to adhere the photo-sensitive chemicals to a glass surface. Once exposed and developed, any number of paper prints could be produced from the glass plate. By 1860 the use of the glass plate negative was virtually universal.[68]

However, the new process possessed serious drawbacks when the camera was taken outside the studio. Equipment was heavy and bulky and the glass plates themselves still required relatively long exposures, weighed a good deal and were susceptible to breakage. A whole season's work in the field could be destroyed in a single mishap. Most importantly of all, wet plate negatives required immediate processing. They had to be sensitized, exposed and developed within thirty minutes before the chemicals hardened. Stoddard, like every other photographer of the period, was burdened not only with cameras and heavy glass plates but with a portable darkroom containing water and all the necessary chemicals (figure 10).[69] William Henry Jackson, one of the era's outstanding landscape photographers, said the following about making wet plate negatives in the field;

> When hard pressed for time, I have made a negative in fifteen minutes, from the time the first rope was thrown from the pack to the final repacking. Ordinarily, however, half an hour was little enough time to do the work well.[70]

The introduction of the dry plate negative in 1880 made the outdoor photographer's life considerably easier. These negatives, usually made in a factory, employed a gelatin emulsion which had the distinct advan-

Figure 10. *AuSable Chasm,* ca. 1870s. Stoddard with his portable darkroom.

tage of remaining photo-sensitive over long periods of time, both before and after exposure.[71] The need for a darkroom in the field was eliminated.

Nonetheless, Stoddard and other outdoor photographers of his day continued to face many difficulties in pursuing their profession. Cameras were still bulky and the glass plate negatives heavy. Stoddard, like the majority of his nineteenth century contemporaries, "contact printed" his images directly onto albumen paper without the benefit of an enlarger. Solar enlargers had been developed in the 1850s but they were expensive, unreliable and rarely used.[72] Stoddard produced a wide range of print sizes from the small *carte de visite* to mammoth plates measuring 14½" by 18½". In order to do so he had to carry different sized cameras and negatives into the field. These difficulties may have contributed to his success. Given the time and effort involved, a photographer was likely to carefully arrange and compose the photograph before exposing the negative.

Stoddard was just one of a number of photographers who began recording the natural environment in the period 1860 to 1885.[73] William Henry Jackson, Timothy O'Sullivan and Carleton Watkins endured even greater hardships in their efforts to photograph the American West.

Several factors contributed to their concern for the wilderness and their willingness to overcome the difficulties inherent in landscape photography. There was a prevailing interest among Americans in nature during the nineteenth century. The discoveries of men like Charles Darwin and Louis Agassiz had been widely disseminated and fostered an awareness of the scientific study of nature.[74] Others saw the hand of God underlying the natural environment and the experience of wilderness as a moral alternative to formal religion.[75] Stoddard, for example, wrote the following about the Adirondacks in 1874;

> . . . pen cannot convey an idea of its sublimity, the pencil fails to even suggest the blended strength and delicacy of the scene. The rude laugh is hushed, the boisterous shout dies on reverential lips, the body shrinks down feeling its own littleness, the soul expands, and rising above the earth, claims kinship with its Creator, questioning not His existence.[76]

Fascination with the American West also drew on a belief that the frontier was a place for new beginnings. As one historian described the attitude, ". . . the West was imagined as a locus of social regeneration and redemption, where tested by the heroic challenge of pioneering, Americans would create a new society closer to nature and to God . . . freed from the corruption and evils of the past."[77] Accordingly, the frontier was as much a process and a place in time as it was a specific geographic location. The Adirondack wilderness, real or imagined, could be easily substituted for the American West. Thus, Stoddard could write of his reasons for visiting the region:

> Does it pay to go through Indian Pass? I answer a thousand times yes. It costs a little extra exertion, but the experiences and emotions of the day come back in a flood of happy recollections, and the soul is lifted a little higher and made better by a visit to that grand old mountain ruin.[78]

These attitudes were particularly evident in the work and philosophies of many American painters of the period. Early in the second quarter of the nineteenth century, a group of American artists, later termed the "Hudson River School," began focusing on the natural environment and produced a large body of landscape paintings.[79] As the century progressed, American landscape painting became increasingly realistic, with particular emphasis placed on the rendering of the effects of natural light. Some scholars have defined this later work as a separate school of painting, called "luminism," and have drawn parallels between luminist painting and the landscape photography of such men as William Henry Jackson, Timothy O'Sullivan, Carleton Watkins and S. R. Stoddard in the period 1860 to 1910.[80]

Although he seems to have shared some of the attitudes of these painters, particularly their religious beliefs about the environment, it is difficult to draw any direct connection between Stoddard and these artists. Stoddard's paintings, of which about twenty are known, do not reflect the luminist style. It does not appear that Stoddard received any formal academic training in art, and he abandoned his work in oils relatively early in his career, by 1880 if not earlier.

It is likely that Stoddard was aware of the work of luminist and landscape photographers. The glass plate negative made their prints readily available, and Stoddard may have learned some of the principles of composition from viewing their images. He displayed his photographs at the Philadelphia Exposition in 1876, and he may have seen the work of such landscape photographers as Charles Bierstadt and Carleton Watkins.[81] Having employed Edward Bierstadt's "artotype" process in 1883, Stoddard was undoubtedly aware of Bierstadt's photographs. He certainly knew William Henry Jackson, for Stoddard included two of Jackson's photographs in his *Picturesque American Resorts,* published in 1892.[82] There is one brief statement in the *Adirondacks Illustrated* in which Stoddard says that some of his views of Ausable Chasm are "actually works of art" (plate 26), one of Stoddard's rare comments concerning how he felt about his photographs.[83]

We must rely, then, on the visual record to establish a connection between Stoddard and paintings of the luminists. Many of Stoddard's landscape photographs share characteristics with these paintings. John Wilmerding found the following luminist qualities in Stoddard's photograph of Little Tupper Lake (figure 11):

> . . . horizontal order, balanced tonal contrasts, open surfaces of silvery water, and low sunlight faced centrally across the views, its reflection a vertical bar perfectly intersecting the shorelines' horizontals.[84]

Many other Stoddard photographs share these features of horizontal composition, calm, placid water and balanced tones (plates 13, 21, 25, 27, 28 and 29).

The use of light was particularly important to luminist art. Stoddard's studies of sunlight and moonlight indicate a similar concern for the effects of light at various times of the day (see figures 11, 12 and 13).

As the natural landscape grew in value in the artist's mind, there was a corresponding reduction in the presence of mankind in luminist art. Often the human figure is either dwarfed by the landscape or is shown in a contemplative relationship to nature.[85] Again, several examples of Stoddard's work can be found to illustrate a similar approach (plates 9, 21, 23 and 30).

However, the evidence can be stretched too far. It is easier to make a case for these features as deliberate conceits of a painter than it is for a photographer. Many of these qualities can just as easily be attributed to the camera as to a conscious effort to produce them. Light is the very heart of the photographic process, and the photographer can hardly avoid recording its effects. Much of

Figure 11. *Little Tupper Lake, Adirondacks,* © 1888.

Figure 12. *Morning,* ca. 1874.

Figure 13. *Moonlight on Lake George,* ca. 1874.

the glassy smoothness of the water in Stoddard's photographs is undoubtedly a result of the technical limitations of his equipment. The relatively long exposures required at the time gave even the rough and tumble movement of a waterfall a milky smooth appearance (figure 14). The horizontal composition that characterizes the majority of his landscapes can easily be attributed to the low horizons of most of his subjects. In sum, Stoddard's work shares some of the attributes of luminist painting but no direct connection can be established between his photographs and the landscape artists of the period.

Figure 14. *Falls of the Raquette below Long Lake,* © 1888.

 Figure 15. *In Fraser Reach, B.C.,* 1892.

We can establish a stronger connection between Stoddard's work and that of his contemporaries in the American West. He was familiar with the photographs of Edward Bierstadt and William Henry Jackson, and his employment on Colvin's scientific expedition and for two Adirondack railroads duplicated assignments of several photographers in the West. Stoddard traveled to the American West in the 1890s and photographed some of the same subjects (figure 15). The Adirondacks, after all, resembled a frontier in size and mystery, as eastern journalists were apt to point out. In 1855, Henry Jarvis Raymond wrote that the Adirondacks were ". . . as unsettled as Nebraska, and less well known than the newest state on the borders of the American Union."[86] And Weston Naef, a photographic historian, sees a distinct parallel: ". . . Stoddard occupies a singular position as the chief counterpart of those working west of the Rocky Mountains."[87] Naef bases this conclusion on Stoddard's images, which echo the work of those photographers in choice of subject and excellence of execution.

Stoddard's overall career must be kept in perspective. He was first and foremost a promoter of the tourist trade and an illustrator of the Adirondacks. His landscapes were just one of the ways in which he portrayed the region. He produced outstanding photographs when he turned the camera's eye upon the Adirondack landscape, and he was among a generation of American photographers who pioneered in the field of landscape photography. As the *Philadelphia Photographer* said of his work in 1876;

> In looking over some of the beautiful views of European scenery, by some of the best artists, we have often sighed for such work by American artists, and now we have it from MR. STODDARD. The stereos are perfect gems of photography, but the larger views captivate us most. They seem to be filled with the feeling and expression of the true artist. For choice of subjects, arrangement, and balance of lines, depth and beauty of perspective, well-chosen and effective foregrounds, and clearly defined yet subdued distance, which with dainty skies give a charming sense of real atmosphere, we have rarely seen these views excelled.[88]

References

1. William H. H. Murray, *Adventures in The Wilderness,* ed. William K. Verner (Syracuse: The Adirondack Museum/ Syracuse University Press, 1970), pp. 5–8.
2. Seneca Ray Stoddard, *Adirondacks Illustrated* (Albany: Weed, Parsons & Co., 1874), pp. 90, 94, 104.
3. Harold P. Smith, *History of Warren County* (Syracuse: D. Mason & Co., 1885), pp. 451–2.
4. *Glens Falls Republican,* August 23, 1864, p. 2.
5. U.S. Bureau of the Census, *Ninth Census of the United States: 1870. Population,* N.Y.S., Warren Co., Town of Queensbury.
6. Adirondack Museum, Stoddard Collection, MS 75-2, Box 7: Scrapbook of newspaper clippings.
7. *Glens Falls Messenger,* May 6, 1870.
8. *Glens Falls Republican,* October 1, 1867, p. 2.
9. Stoddard, *Lake George: (Illustrated)* (Albany: Weed Parsons & Co., 1874), p. 200.
10. William Welling, *Collectors Guide to Nineteenth Century Photographs* (New York: MacMillan Publishing Co., 1976), p. 78.
11. *Lake George; (Illustrated),* 1873, p. 86.
12. Adirondack Museum, sketchbook, 1870, 74.233.45.
13. *Glens Falls Republican,* November 15, 1870, p. 3.
14. *Watertown Times,* November 6, 1966.
15. *Adirondacks Illustrated,* 1876, back page.
16. *Glens Falls Republican,* October 1, 1867, p. 2.
17. *List of Photographs of 1874* (Glens Falls: S. R. Stoddard, 1875).
18. *Lake George; (Illustrated),* 1874, p. 200.
19. *Glens Falls Republican,* May 27, 1884, p. 3.
20. MS 75-2, Box 8: Account Books 1872–1879 and 1879–1914.
21. Verplank Colvin, *Seventh Annual Report on the Progress of the Topographical Survey of the Adirondack Region of New York to the Year 1879,* State of New York (Albany: Weed, Parsons & Co., Printers, 1880), pp. 40, 60–61, 353.
22. MS 75-2, Box 1, Folder 6: Letter from A. T. Stoddard to Maitland DeSormo, August 4, 1961.
23. American Canoe Association, *Year Book: 1892* (Albany: Riggs Printing & Publishing Co., 1892).
24. Adirondack Museum, Durant Collection, MS 63-258, Letter Book: William W. Durant to S. R. Stoddard, July 3, 6 and August 23, 1899, June 5 and 26, 1900.
25. Ibid.

    MS 75-2: Account Book 1879–1914, p. 536.
26. *Albany Daily Argus,* February 26, 1892.
27. State of New York: *Annual Reports of the Forest Commission,* 1891 and 1893 (Albany: James B. Lyon, State Printer, 1891 and 1894).
28. MS 75-2: Account Book 1879–1914, p. 158.
29. "Among the Balsams," *Harper's Weekly,* XXXII (August 11, 1888), p. 597.

    "Adirondack Woods, Waters and Camps," *Frank Leslie's Illustrated Newspaper,* (August 13, 1887), p. 417.
30. Stoddard, *Picturesque American Resorts* (Glens Falls: S. R. Stoddard, 1892), title page.
31. Stoddard, *Lake George: Photographs* (Glens Falls: S. R. Stoddard, 1886).
32. *Glens Falls Messenger,* August 2, 1878, p. 3.
33. Stoddard, *Lake George* (Glens Falls: S. R. Stoddard, 1883), title page.
34. Robert Taft, *Photography and the American Scene* (New York: Dover Publications, Inc., 1964), pp. 431, 513.
35. *St. Johns Globe,* August 5, 1886.

36. *Glens Falls Republican,* February 12, 1891.

37. MS 75-2, Box 1, Folders 4 and 5: Patent no. 257408, and pamphlet for "Stoddard Combination Plate and Film Holder."

38. MS 75-2: Account Book 1879–1914, pp. 81, 85, 88, 237, 322, 414.

39. *Adirondacks Illustrated,* 1906, pp. 249, 274.

40. MS 75-2: Account Book 1872–1879, p. 28.

41. MS 75-2, Box 7: Field notes for *Adirondacks Illustrated,* 1873.

42. *Adirondacks Illustrated,* 1874, p. 38.

43. Ibid., p. 89.

44. *A History of the Adirondacks,* Vol. I (Harrison, N.Y.: Harbor Hill Books, 1977), p. 208.

45. *Lake George; (Illustrated),* 1894, pp. 146, 177.

46. Adirondack Mountain Club, *Adirondack Bibliography,* Vol. I (Gabriels, N.Y.: Adirondack Mountain Club, Inc., 1958), pp. 41–2.

47. *Adirondacks Illustrated,* 1880, pp. xiii–xiv, 7–8.

48. *History,* Vol. I, p. 208.

49. Stoddard, *Map of the Adirondacks* (Glens Falls: S. R. Stoddard, 1912).

50. MS 75-2: Account Book 1879–1914, p. 530.

51. Stoddard, *Map of Lake George* (Glens Falls: S. R. Stoddard, 1884).

52. Smith, *History,* p. 452.

53. *Glens Falls Messenger,* March 28, 1890, p. 2.

54. Stoddard, *Chart of Lake George* (Glens Falls: S. R. Stoddard, 1910).

55. *Stoddard's Northern Monthly,* II (June, 1907), p. 133.

56. *Glens Falls Republican,* February 12, 1891.

57. MS 75-2, Box 1, Folder 3: Pamphlet, "Major J. B. Pond, Lecturers and Their Subjects: Entertainers and Readers, Season of 1901–1902."

58. MS 75-2: Account Book 1879–1914, p. 204.

59. MS 75-2, Box 1, Folder 3: Circulars, "The Florida Chautauqua: DeFuniak Springs, Florida," 1900–1902.

60. *Albany Daily Argus,* February 26, 1892.

61. "The Headwaters of the Hudson," *Outing,* VII (October, 1885), pp. 58–63.

62. *Adirondacks Illustrated,* 1897, p. vii. *Adirondacks Illustrated,* 1901, p. ix.

63. *Stoddard's Northern Monthly,* I (October, 1906), back cover.

64. "Vale," *Stoddard's Northern Monthly,* IV, (September, 1908), pp. 198–206.

65. *New York Mail and Express,* June 9, 1894.

66. A. L. Stoddard (ed.), *Stoddard and Spencer's Directory and Map of Glens Falls, N.Y.* (Glens Falls: Stoddard and Spencer, Publishers, 1874), p. 67.

67. Weston J. Naef and James N. Wood, *Era of Exploration: The Rise of Landscape Photography in the American West, 1860–1885* (Boston: New York Graphic Society, 1975), pp. 13–14.

68. Larry Booth and Robert A. Weinstein, *Collection, Use and Care of Historic Photographs* (Nashville: American Association for State and Local History, 1977), pp. 6–7, 208.

69. Doug Munson and Joel Snyder, *The Documentary Photograph as a Work of Art; American Photographs, 1860–1867* (Chicago: The David and Alfred Smart Gallery, 1976), pp. 33–4.

70. Ibid., p. 25.

71. Booth and Weinstein, pp. 7, 208.

72. Karen Current, *Photography and the Old West* (New York: Harry N. Abrams, Inc., 1978), pp. 24–5.

73. Naef and Wood, p. 12.

74. Ibid., pp. 16–17.

75. Barbara Novak, *Nature and Culture: American Landscape and Painting, 1825–1875* (New York: Oxford University Press, 1980), p. 20.

76. *Adirondacks Illustrated,* 1874, p. 2.

77. Munson and Snyder, p. 27.

78. *Adirondacks Illustrated,* 1874, p. 130.

79. John K. Howat, *The Hudson River and Its Painters* (New York: Penguin Books, 1972). p. 27.

80. Weston Naef, "New Eyes — Luminism and Photography," in John Wilmerding, *American Light: The Luminist Movement, 1850–1875* (Washington, D.C.: The National Gallery of Art, 1980), p. 288.

81. United States Centennial Commission, *International Exhibition, 1876. Official Catalogue: Department of Art* (Philadelphia: John R. Nagle and Company, 1876), pp. 55–8.

82. *Picturesque Resorts.*

83. *Adirondacks Illustrated,* 1874, p. 51.

84. Wilmerding, p. 143.

85. Novak, p. 193.

86. *The New-York Daily Times,* June 19, 1855.

87. Wilmerding, p. 283.

88. Stoddard, *Catalogue of Photographs of New York Scenery* (Glens Falls: S. R. Stoddard, 1877), p. 13.

Figure 16. The Narrows, Lake George, ca. 1870s.

Figure 17. *Blue Mountain Lake, Oct. 11, 1873.*

Figure 18. *Map of the Adirondack Wilderness, Compiled by S. R. Stoddard, Eighth (Revised) Edition, 1887.*

Figure 20. Cover for *Stoddard's Northern Monthly,* May, 1906.

Figure 19. *(Left)* Cover for *The Adirondacks: Illustrated,* 1874, printer's proof.

Plate 1. *Adirondack R.R. bridge across the Sacondaga,* n.d.

Plate 2. Fort William Henry Hotel, Lake George, n.d.

Plate 3. *Bridge at Outlet Blue Mountain Lake, Adirondacks,* © 1889.

Plate 4. *Raquette River. At Sweeney Carry,* © 1888.

Plate 5. *Fort William Henry Hotel Piazza from West,* n.d.

Plate 6. *Blue Mountain Lake House, Adirondacks,* © 1889.

Plate 7. *Upper Saranac Lake. On the Sweeney Carry,* © 1889.

Plate 8. *Restaurant, at Marion River Carry,* n.d.

Plate 9. *Horicon Sketching Club, 1882.*

Plate 10. *Paddling Race 1885. "Viva," "Bijou," "Maggie."*

 Plate 11. *"In the Adirondacks." Adirondacks,* © 1889.

Plate 12. *Bridge at Lake Colden, Adirondacks,* n.d.

Plate 13. *Haystack Mountain, From Upper AuSable Pond,* ca. 1878.

Plate 14. *Game in the Adirondacks,* © 1889.

Plate 15. *Alva Dunning, Adirondack Guide and Hunter,* © 1891.

Plate 16. William West Durant, Camp Pine Knot, n.d.

Plate 17. *Summer,* View at North Elba, n.d.

Plate 18. *Lumbering in the Adirondacks. The Choppers,* © 1888.

 Plate 19. *Charcoal Kilns, The Narrows. Chateaugay Lake,* © 1891.

Plate 20. *Clinton Prison. Prisoners and Keepers,* ca. 1874.

 Plate 21. *Avalanche Lake, Adirondacks,* © 1888.

Plate 22. *Sentinel Rock, head of lower Saranac Lake,* n.d.

 Plate 23. *The Adirondacks. Keene Valley from Prospect Hill,* © 1887.

Plate 24. Unidentified Landscape, n.d.

Plate 25. *Sagamore Lodge. From South Inlet Falls Road, 1899.*

Plate 26. *Ausable Chasm — Up the River from Table Rock,* n.d.

Plate 27. *Lower AuSable Lake, Adirondacks,* © 1889.

Plate 28. *The Adirondacks. Upper AuSable Lake from Boreas Bay,* © 1887.

Plate 29. *Lake "Tear of the Clouds," Adirondacks,* n.d.

Plate 30. *Drowned Lands of the Lower Raquette, Adirondacks,* © 1888.

Checklist of the Exhibition

Unless otherwise noted, all items listed below are from the collections of the Adirondack Museum. Artifacts preceded by an asterisk (*) are illustrated in the catalog. Titles in italics are Stoddard's titles.

PHOTOGRAPHS

*1. *Avalanche Lake, Adirondacks,* © 1888, albumen print, 14½″ × 18½″ (plate 21).
*2. *"In the Adirondacks." Adirondacks,* © 1889, albumen print, 14½″ × 18½″ (plate 11).
*3. Unidentified Landscape, n.d., albumen print, 14″ × 10″ (plate 24).
*4. *Sentinel Rock, head of lower Saranac Lake,* n.d., albumen print, 10″ × 14″ (plate 22).
5. *The Adirondacks. Cascade at Edmonds Pond,* n.d., albumen print, 14½″ × 18½″.
6. *Birmingham Falls from above,* n.d., albumen print, 13″ × 9½″.
7. *Paul Smith's, St. Regis Lake, Adirondacks,* n.d., albumen print, 5″ × 14″.
*8. *Ausable Chasm — Up the River from Table Rock,* n.d., albumen print, 13½″ × 10½″ (plate 26).
*9. *Lower AuSable Lake, Adirondacks,* © 1889, albumen print, 14½″ × 18½″ (plate 27).
*10. *The Adirondacks. Upper AuSable Lake from Boreas Bay,* © 1887, albumen print, 14½″ × 18½″ (plate 28).
*11. *Lake "Tear of the Clouds," Adirondacks,* n.d., albumen print, 14½″ × 18½″ (plate 29).
*12. *The Adirondacks. Keene Valley from Prospect Hill,* © 1887, albumen print, 14½″ × 18½″ (plate 23).
*13. *Sagamore Lodge. From South Inlet Falls Road,* 1899, albumen print, 14½″ × 18½″ (plate 25).
14. *Adirondack Hunters at Night,* © 1888, albumen print, 14½″ × 18½″.
*15. *Drowned Lands of the Lower Raquette, Adirondacks,* © 1888, albumen print, 14½″ × 18½″ (plate 30).
16. Bedroom, Camp Pine Knot, n.d., albumen print, 6½″ × 8½″.
*17. William West Durant, Camp Pine Knot, n.d., albumen print, 6½″ × 8½″ (plate 16).
*18. Fort William Henry Hotel, Lake George, n.d., albumen print, 4¼″ × 7½″ (plate 2).
19. *Fleet of the Champlain Transportation Company,* n.d., albumen print, 6¼″ × 8″.
*20. *Bridge at Outlet of Blue Mountain Lake, Adirondacks,* © 1889, albumen print, 4¼″ × 7½″ (plate 3).
*21. *Horicon Sketching Club, 1882,* albumen print, 4¼″ × 7½″ (plate 9).
*22. *Fort William Henry Hotel Piazza from west,* n.d., albumen print, 4½″ × 7½″ (plate 5).
*23. *Summer,* n.d., albumen print, 4½″ × 7½″ (plate 17).

*24. *Adirondack R.R. bridge across the Sacondaga,* n.d., albumen print, 4½″ × 7½″ (plate 1).

*25. *Restaurant, at Marion River Carry,* n.d., albumen print, 4½″ × 7½″ (plate 8).

26. *An Adirondack House,* n.d., albumen print, 4½ ″ × 7½″.

27. Village of Ticonderoga, n.d., albumen print, 10″ × 58¾″.

*28. *Game in the Adirondacks,* © 1889, albumen print, 6½″ × 8½″ (plate 14).

*29. *Clinton Prison. Prisoners and Keepers,* ca. 1874, albumen print, 6½″ × 8½″ (plate 20).

*30. *Lumbering in the Adirondacks. The Choppers,* © 1888, albumen print, 6½″ × 8½″ (plate 18).

*31. *Charcoal Kilns, The Narrows. Chateaugay Lake,* © 1891, albumen print, 6½″ × 8½″ (plate 19).

32. *Adirondack Lumber Shanty — A good story,* © 1888, albumen print, 6½″ × 8½″.

33. *Raquette River; Canal into Simon's Pond,* © 1888, albumen print, 6½″ × 8½″.

*34. *Upper Saranac Lake. On the Sweeney Carry,* © 1889, albumen print, 6½″ × 8½″ (plate 7).

*35. *Bridge at Lake Colden, Adirondacks,* n.d., albumen print, 6½″ × 8½″ (plate 12).

*36. *Raquette River. At Sweeney Carry,* © 1888, albumen print, 6½″ × 8½″ (plate 4).

37. *Adirondack R.R. Survey Party near Long Lake,* 1888, albumen print, 6½″ × 8½″.

38. *A.C.A. Camp,* 1887, albumen print, 4½″ × 7½″.

*39. *Paddling Race 1885. "Viva," "Bijou," "Maggie,"* 1885, albumen print, 4½ ″ × 7½ ″(plate 10).

*40. *Blue Mountain Lake House, Adirondacks,* © 1889, albumen print, 6½″ × 8½″ (plate 6).

41. *Blue Mountain Lake from the Mountain House,* © 1889, albumen print, 6½″ × 8½″.

42. *Blue Mountain House,* © 1889, albumen print, 6½″ × 8½″.

43. *A Toiler of the Sea* (Seneca Ray Stoddard), ca. 1891, albumen print, 6½″ × 8½″.

*44. *Alva Dunning, Adirondack Guide and Hunter,* © 1891, albumen print, 8½″ × 6½″ (plate 15).

*45. *Haystack Mountain, from Upper Ausable Pond,* ca. 1878, stereograph, 4″ × 6″ (plate 13).

46. *Adirondack Photographs, Vol. 1, William West Durant,* ca. 1889, presentation album, 19″ × 24″, 37 albumen prints, 14½″ × 18½″. Gift of Mr. & Mrs. Adam Hochschild. (The existence of volume two is unknown.)

47. *Sagamore Park in the Adirondacks,* 1899, album, 11″ × 14″, 40 photographs, various sizes.

48. *Lake George Illustrated,* n.d., 24 page sales album, 20″ × 17″.

49. *Lake George, Steamer Adirondack,* n.d., 22 page sales album, 20½″ × 17″.

50–61. Lantern slides, ca. 1891, 3¼ ″ × 4″.
Mitchell Sabattis.
Foquets Hotel, Plattsburgh.
Tent Suite, Ampersand Hotel, Lower Saranac.
Hurricane Pass.
John Brown's Grave.
Whiteface Mountain Summit.
Carrying a Guide Boat.
Avalanche Lake Bridge.
Raquette Lake.
View from the Stern Seat.
Alvah Dunning.
Absorbed.

SKETCHES, DRAWINGS AND ILLUSTRATIONS

62. *Long Lake South, Oct. 4th 1870,* pencil sketch on paper, 4¾″ × 7″. (This sketch was the basis for an oil painting, catalog number 100.)

63. Whiteface Mountain from North Elba, 1873, pencil sketch on paper, 6½″ × 8¼″.

64. High Peaks, Adirondacks, 1873, pencil sketch on paper, 6½ ″ × 17″. (This sketch was the basis of a pen and ink illustration for *The Adirondacks: Illustrated.*)

65. Sketchbook, 1866, sixteen pencil sketches on paper, 4″ × 5¼″.

66. Sketchbook, 1869, nine pencil sketches on paper, 4″ × 8½″.

67. Sketchbook, 1870, twenty-seven pencil sketches on paper and one albumen print, 7½″ × 7″.

68. Sketchbook, 1872, sixteen pencil sketches on paper, 3½″ × 5½″.

*69. Sketchbook, 1873, nineteen pencil sketches on paper, 6¾″ × 8½″ (figure 17).

70. Blue Mountain Lake House, Adirondacks, ca. 1889, pen and ink drawing on paper, 8½″ × 9″.

71. Blue Mountain Lake from the Mountain House, ca. 1889, pen and ink drawing on paper, 7¼″ × 13″.

72. Blue Mountain House, ca. 1889, pen and ink drawing on paper, 6¼″ × 9½″.

73. A Toiler of the Sea, (Seneca Ray Stoddard), ca. 1891, pen and ink drawing on paper, 4¾″ × 8½″.

74–90. *The Adirondacks: Illustrated,* 1872–1873, seventeen pen and ink drawings on illustration board, various sizes.

*91. *The Adirondacks: Illustrated,* 1874, twenty-nine wood engravings, bound volume of printer's proofs, 7″ × 4¼″ (figure 19).

92. *Adirondack Woods, Waters and Camps,* nine wood engravings after Stoddard photographs, 16″ × 10¾″ *(Frank Leslie's Illustrated Newspaper,* August 13, 1887).

93. *Views in the Adirondacks,* nine wood engravings after Stoddard photographs, 9½″ × 14½″ (*Harper's Weekly,* August 11, 1888).

94. Photographic montage, 1892, fifty-five "phototype views" from *Picturesque American Resorts* (catalog number 131), 18½″ × 10½″. Lent by Wildwood Enterprises.

95. *Alvah Dunning,* 1892, copper plate etching on paper, by Arpad G. Gerster, after Stoddard photograph (catalog number 44), 5½″ × 5½″. Gift of Dr. John C. A. Gerster.

PAINTINGS

96. *In the Drowned Lands of the Raquette River,* ca. 1870s, monochrome oil on academy board, 5½″ × 8″.

97. Mount Marcy across Wolf Pond, ca. 1870s, monochrome oil on academy board, circular, 6½″ in diameter.

98. Along the Upper Hudson, ca. 1870s, monochrome oil on academy board, 2¼″ × 7½″.

99. Mountain Trail in the Adirondacks, ca. 1870s, monochrome oil on academy board, 9½″ × 2½″.

100. Long Lake, 1870, oil on canvas, 4¼″ × 7¼″. Lent by Mr. & Mrs. W. K. Verner. (See catalog number 62 for matching pencil sketch.)

101. Summit Rock, Indian Pass, ca. 1870s, oil on canvas, 6¼″ × 8¼″.

102. Keene Valley from Baxter Mountain, ca. 1870s, oil on canvas, 6¼″ × 8¼″.

103. Adirondack Lakeshore, ca. 1870s, oil on academy board, 7¼″ × 9¾″.

*104. The Narrows, Lake George, ca. 1870s, oil on academy board, 8½″ × 13½″. Gift of Carl E. Plumley Memorial Fund (figure 16).

105. View of the Hudson near Newcomb, ca. 1870s, oil on academy board, 8¼″ × 10¾″.

106. Keene Valley, 1877, oil on canvas, 14″ × 30″. Lent by Mr. & Mrs. Robert Worth.

107. Sugarloaf Mountain, ca. 1880, oil on canvas, 12″ × 22″, by Henry Suydam after Stoddard stereograph (catalog number 45).

MAPS

108. *Map of the New York Wilderness: accompanying "The Adirondacks Illustrated,"* 1874, prepared by G. W. & C. B. Colton & Co., 25″ × 21″ (shows the route of Stoddard's 1873 trip to the Adirondacks).

*109. *Map of the Adirondack Wilderness,* 1888, tenth revised edition, printed for the New York Forest Commission, 31″ × 25″ (see figure 18).

110. *Map of Lake George,* 1899, eighth revised edition, 36½″ × 10½″.

111. *Map of Lake Champlain,* 1911, twelfth revised edition, 36½″ × 10½″.

112. *Stoddard's Auto-Roadmap of the Adirondacks, the Champlain Valley and the Hudson River,* 1910, 34″ × 20″.

113. *Chart of Lake George: Hydrographic Survey of 1906-7-8,* 1910, 98″ × 15″.

114. Cover for *Map of the Adirondacks,* 1884, fifth revised edition, 6¾″ × 4¼″.

115. Cover for *Map of the Adirondack Lands, The Forest Commission, State of New York,* ca. 1888, 9⅛″ × 5½″.

116. Cover for *Stoddard's Illustrated Auto-Road Map of the Adirondacks, The Champlain Valley and the Hudson River,* ca. 1910, 4⅝″ × 10⅜″.

117. Cover for *Stoddard's Map of Lake Champlain,* 1911, 5½″ × 3½″.

118. Cover for *Stoddard's Map of Lake George,* 1913, 5½″ × 4″.

119. Printer's block for *Stoddard's Map of the Adirondacks,* n.d., metal engraving plate on wood, 5″ × 4¼″.

PUBLICATIONS

120. *Lake George; (Illustrated),* Glens Falls, N.Y.: S. R. Stoddard, 1873, 7¾″ × 4¾″.

121. *Ticonderoga: Past and Present,* Glens Falls, N.Y.: S. R. Stoddard, 1873, 7¾″ × 4½″.

122. *Lake George; (Illustrated),* Glens Falls, N.Y.: S. R. Stoddard, 1874, 7½″ × 4¾″.

123. *Catalog of Photographs of New York Scenery,* Glens Falls, N.Y.: S. R. Stoddard, 1877, 7″ × 5¾″.

124. *The Adirondacks,* Glens Falls, N.Y.: S. R. Stoddard, 1878, thirty-two lithographs, 3¼″ × 5″.

125. *Lake George,* Glens Falls, N.Y.: S. R. Stoddard, 1883, twelve artotype illustrations by Edward Bierstadt, 7″ × 7″.

126. *The Adirondacks: Illustrated,* Glens Falls, N.Y.: S. R. Stoddard, 1884, 7″ × 4½″.

127. *Saratoga,* New York: Adolph Vitterman, 1885, fourteen lithographs after Stoddard photographs, 3½″ × 5″.

128. *Lake George,* New York: Adolph Vitterman, 1885, twelve lithographs after Stoddard photographs, 3½″ × 5″.

129. *The Adirondacks: Illustrated,* Glens Falls, N.Y.: S. R. Stoddard, 1888 (with Stoddard's revisions for 1889), 7″ × 4½″.

130. *The Adirondacks: Illustrated,* Glens Falls, N.Y.: S. R. Stoddard, 1891 (presentation copy given to W. W. Durant with "compliments of S. R. Stoddard"), 7½″ × 5″.

131. *Picturesque American Resorts,* Glens Falls, N.Y.: S. R. Stoddard, 1892, 11″ × 14″.

132. *Camp Life,* Boston: Joseph Knight Company, ca. 1892, twelve photogravures after Stoddard photographs, 9½″ × 11½″.

133. *The Cruise of the Friesland, 1895,* Glens Falls, N.Y.: S. R. Stoddard, 1896 (number 190 of 200 copies), 10¼″ × 8½″.

134. *Bits of Adirondack Life,* Glens Falls, N.Y.: S. R. Stoddard, 1898, 6¾″ × 9¼″.
135. *Historic Lake Champlain,* Glens Falls, N.Y.: S. R. Stoddard, 1898, 6¾″ × 9¼″.
136. *Into the Lake Region,* Glens Falls, N.Y.: S. R. Stoddard, 1900, 6½″ × 9¼″.
*137. *Stoddard's Northern Monthly,* Glens Falls, N.Y.: S. R. Stoddard, May, 1906, 10″ × 6⅞″ (figure 20).
138. *AuSable Chasm,* Glens Falls, N.Y.: S. R. Stoddard, 1907, 6¼″ × 4″.
139. *Lake George and Lake Champlain; (Illustrated),* Glens Falls, N.Y.: S. R. Stoddard, 1915, 5¾″ × 4½″.
140. *Picturesque Trips Through the Adirondacks in an Automobile,* Glens Falls, N.Y.: S. R. Stoddard, 1915, 10″ × 5″.

MANUSCRIPTS

141. Journal of Stoddard's trip to Adirondacks, with field notes for *The Adirondacks: Illustrated,* September and October, 1873, 6¼″ × 4″.
142. Handwritten manuscript page for *The Adirondacks: Illustrated,* 1873, 12½″ × 8″.
143–144. Advertising cards seeking information for *The Adirondacks: Illustrated* from the Saranac Club House and the Hotel Wawbeek, n.d., 5½″ × 3¼″.
145. Patent number 257408, issued to Seneca R. Stoddard for "Photographic Apparatus," May 2, 1882.
146. Sales brochure for "The Stoddard Combination Plate and Film Holder," manufactured by E. L. Elliot & Co., Auburn, N.Y., n.d., 4½″ × 5⅞″.
147. Copyright number 17019T, issued to S. R. Stoddard for *Map of Lake George,* June 14, 1888.
148. Unpublished manuscript, *The Story of Atlantis,* 319 typed pages in two volumes with sketches, 1890, 10½″ × 8″.
149. Advertising circular for "S. R. Stoddard's Illustrated Lectures" under the management of Major J. B. Pond, N.Y., four page brochure, ca. 1900, 5¾″ × 3¾″.
150. Advertising circular for "S. R. Stoddard" under the management of Star Lyceum Bureau, four pages, ca. 1900, 11½″ × 8¼″.
151. Business card, "S. R. Stoddard, Glens Falls, N.Y.," ca. 1906, 2″ × 3½″.

Chronology: SENECA RAY STODDARD

1843 Born May 13, in the Town of Wilton, Saratoga County, N.Y.

1862 Moves to Troy, N.Y. and works as an ornamental painter of railroad cars for the Eaton & Gilbert Car Works.

1864 Moves to Glens Falls, N.Y. and opens a shop for "House, Sign and Ornamental Painting."

1867 First notice of Stoddard as a landscape photographer appears in a Glens Falls newspaper.

1868 Marries Helen Augusta Potter.

1870 Makes first trip to the central Adirondacks, recording the landscape with camera and sketches. Listed as a "landscape painter" in the census and offers art lessons in his studio.

1873 Publishes his first two guidebooks: *Lake George; (Illustrated)* and *Ticonderoga: Past and Present.* Makes his second trip through the central Adirondacks. The narrative of this journey will serve as the basis of his Adirondack guidebook for nearly twenty years.

1874 Publishes the first edition of his guidebook, *The Adirondacks: Illustrated.* Listed in a Glens Falls directory as a "landscape photographer." Publishes his *Map of the New York Wilderness* based on W. W. Ely's 1867 map.

1875 Publishes his first catalog of photographs, *List of Photographs of 1874.*

1876 Exhibits photographs at the Philadelphia Centennial Exposition.

1878 In charge of the photographic division of the N.Y. State Topographical Survey of the Adirondacks. Publishes *The Adirondacks,* the first of a series of view books employing photomechanical reproduction.

1880 Publishes his *Map of the Adirondack Wilderness* and conducts a survey of Lake George.

1881 Probable publication date of his *Map of Lake George.* Photographs the route of the New York and Canadian Railroad.

1882 Granted patent for a "combination plate and film holder," later manufactured by E. L. Elliot and Co., Auburn, N.Y.

1883 Begins the first leg of a canoe voyage from Lake George to St. Johns, New Brunswick, completed the summer of 1886.

1888 Special edition of the *Map of the Adirondack Wilderness* printed for the New York State Forest Commission.

1890 Publishes his *Map of Lake Champlain.*

1891 Gives his first illustrated lecture, "A Canoe Trip to the Bay of Fundy."

1892 Addresses the New York State Assembly on February 25th to support the creation of an "Adirondack Park," then tours the state presenting the same illustrated lecture. Legislation creating the Park was approved May 20, 1892. Travels to Alaska.

1894 Travels across the American West.

1895 Travels to the Mediterranean and the Near East.

1897 Travels to Great Britain, the North Atlantic, Russia and Scandinavia. Granted patent for "improvements to electric trolleys."

1900 Travels to Germany and France and visits the Paris Exposition.

1906 His first wife dies. Publishes the first issue of *Stoddard's Northern Monthly* in May. Begins surveys for his hydrographic chart of Lake George.

1908 Marries his second wife, Emily Doty. Last issue of his magazine published in September.

1909 Publishes completed version of his *Chart of Lake George.*

1910 Probable publication date of his *Auto-Road Map of the Adirondacks, the Champlain Valley and the Hudson River.*

1917 Dies May 3.